The Keys to Success

Written by
Cedric Jones

PublishAmerica
Baltimore

© 2012 by Cedric Jones.
All rights reserved. No part of this book may be reproduced, stored in a retrieval system or transmitted in any form or by any means without the prior written permission of the publishers, except by a reviewer who may quote brief passages in a review to be printed in a newspaper, magazine or journal.

First printing

PublishAmerica has allowed this work to remain exactly as the author intended, verbatim, without editorial input.

Softcover 9781627090667
PUBLISHED BY PUBLISHAMERICA, LLLP
www.publishamerica.com
Baltimore

Printed in the United States of America

Dedication

I dedicate this book to my Lord and Savior Jesus Christ who is the reason for my very existence. I am nothing without you. I love and appreciate you for all you have done in my life. No words could ever really express my gratitude for the love, patience, and grace you have bestowed upon me. I would not be here today had it not been for you. Thank you! I also dedicate this book to "Life" for beating up on me, teaching me humility and most importantly for chasing me into the presence of God. I dedicate this book to my mother who has always loved and supported me unconditionally. I thank you Lord for my pastor and the prophets you used to speak my destiny into the earth realm; for the intercessors who have lifted me up in prayer and to those who have spoken encouraging words to lift me up when I was feeling down. Thank you all.

Introduction

I am writing this book as a testimony to the goodness of God. I would like to submit to my readers this day that absolutely everything I have tried to do in my own strength has failed. Through my many trials and tribulations I have come to realization that I am helpless and hopeless without God. It was not until God began to speak prophetically into my life that the course of my life began to change. *Amos 3:7.* I would begin a thing but would never be able to finish it. I would start a job but only keep it six months. I signed up with the U.S. Army Reserves but only served a year before being placed in the I.R.R. (Individual Ready Reserves). I attempted college enrollment several times but never made it past the first semester. I moved from state to state several times only to end up back at home within three to six months. It was not until I surrendered my life to God that I experience any real success.

We were taught in school that in order to be successful one had to finish college and earn a degree. We were taught a rhyme in math class that went: *"The name of the game is money. The more you learn, the more you earn.* So I set out on my quest to learn so that I could earn. Many people I know have gone on to do just that. They have finished college and have gone on to receive their Master's and PhD's. Yet for some reason there were giant boulders standing in the way of me achieving my success. I've sought success all of my life. I've tried the world's ideology of success and found out that for some reason those rules do not apply to my life. It took many years of bumping my head over and over and over again to realize that my plan was flawed.

I once read somewhere that the definition of insanity is doing the same thing over and over again but expecting different results. I must admit that I had to be one of the most insane people alive. I had tried **"MY WAY"** over and over and over and over again until finally I came to the conclusion that *MY WAY is not working!*

Realizing God had a plan for my life has made all the difference. According to Jeremiah 29:11, not only does God have a plan for my life, but He has a plan that will prosper me and bring me to a desired end. God wants me to succeed, so much so that He's at work helping me do it. I've learned that it is impossible to walk with God and not walk into your destiny. The success that I was seeking was found in God all along.

Contents

Dedication 3
Introduction 4
Key #1 9
Keep God First
Key #2 13
Never Quit
Key #3 19
Walk in Humility
Key #4 22
Take One Step at a Time
Key #5 25
Allow angels to work on your behalf
Key #6 30
Don't worry about things you have no control over
Key #7 34
Trust in God's Provision
Key #8 37
Stay in God's Will
Key #9 40
Get out of God's Way
Key #10 43
Know that you can do it
Key #11 52
Have the proper mindset
Key #12 56
Learn to ask for help

The Keys to Success

Key #1
Keep God First

Matthew 6:33 But seek ye first the kingdom of God and His righteousness and all these things shall be added to you.

The first key to success is to keep God first. If you are deciding to go back to school after many years, chances are you have responsibilities like a job, a family, or a business and you must learn how to balance everything so one won't outweigh the other. Life can get quite busy and hectic. Some days you don't know whether you are coming or going. But whatever you do do not put God on the back burner. The bible says *"that God holds king's hearts in the hands of the Lord, as the rivers of water; He turneth it whithersoever He will"*. *Proverbs 21:1.* If a choice has to be made between school attendance and church attendance always go with God.

After spending about a year at Stonecliff College online "Life" happened. I will explain what I mean about "life" in the next chapter. I began working a job at a factory on the graveyard shift. I hadn't gotten used to the hours yet and trying to develop a new sleep pattern, handle responsibilities at home, go to school, and still maintain my spiritual responsibilities was overwhelming. A decision had to be made: (1) I had to work because I had bills to pay II *Thessalonians 3:10.* (2)

I had to take care of responsibilities around the house. The only things left were school and God and I had to make a choice. I chose God and let school go for the time being. After working about eight months at the factory we were laid off and I found myself in the unemployment line. At the time I received a prophetic word from a minister that God was going to cause me to matriculate in the education system. I had no idea what the word matriculate meant so when I made it home later that evening I looked it up. Matriculate means to enroll in a college or University. God was right on time! Around the same time my former boss from McCarty's of Pottery walked up to me at a local convenience store and told me that a person just left and they had a job opening available. I was then told to hurry up and get my resume in before someone else applies for the position. I was rehired on the spot.

After receiving the prophetic word about school I decided to try and enroll at a local Community College in Clarksdale, MS. This was perfect because they offered evening classes at the high school in my hometown from 6:00 to 9:00 p.m. I could go to work during the day, get off at 4:00 p.m. and still have time to make it to class at 6:00 p.m.

The easy part was making the decision to enroll at the community college. The hard part was I had no clue as to how to begin. There were signs posted on the lawn of the high school's campus announcing the time and date of registration and I decided to go on the first night to enroll. I was totally lost but I went anyway. I prayed and prayed *"Lord please order my steps. I'm lost. I don't even know where to begin but I'm going to this registration."* I went in and filled out all the registration forms I was told to fill out. Then I turned them in and left it at that. About a week had past and I thought about it more but hadn't quite made the decision to go to the campus to complete registration. I was slowly putting it off until the next semester. One evening after I made it home from work I received a phone call from one of the women that was in charge of registration at the high school the evening I went to register. She said "Mr. Jones are you going to complete registration?" I said "I don't think so. I may just wait until next semester." Then she asked "what's keeping you from registering this semester?" I said honestly "I don't know." She said "Mr. Jones just come on down to the campus this evening and we'll get you settled. I went to campus that evening and this woman walked right up to me as soon as I walked in the door. She took my paper work, walked me through financial aid and the next thing I knew I was registered for classes. From that point on I just showed up for registration. I probably couldn't tell you today the registration process because I always just showed up. I think its called providence; I'm where I'm supposed to be at a particular time and everything just unfolds from that point on.

There have also been times when our bible study nights would change from Wednesday night to Thursday nights during the month of January. This presented another dilemma for me. I had to make a choice between missing school and missing church on Thursday nights. I chose to miss school. I prayed about it then I went to my instructor and explained my situation and asked could I leave early on Thursday evenings so I could get to bible studies by 7:00 p.m. She said she had no problem as long as I could keep up with the work. Next I asked my pastor if it would be okay if I missed the first hour of praise and worship on Thursday night to attend school. She said that it would be perfect. I would make it to church just in time for the Word. I put God first and ended up getting an "A" in the class.

Key #2

Never Quit

Quitting is Not an Option

Don't Quit Poem

When things go wrong as they sometimes will,
When the road you're trudging seems all uphill
When the funds are low and the debts are high,
And you want to smile, but you have to sigh,
When care is pressing you down a bit --
Rest if you must, but don't quit.

Life is strange with its twists and turns,
As every one of us sometimes learns,
And many a fellow turns about
When he might have won had he stuck it out.
Don't give up though the pace seems slow --
You may succeed with another blow.

Often the goal is nearer than
It seems to a fair and faltering man,
Often the struggler has given up
When he might have captured the victor's cup,
And he learned too late when night came down,
How close he was to the golden crown.

Success is failure turned inside out --
The silver tint of the clouds of doubt,
And you never can tell how close you are,
It may be near when it seems afar,
So stick to the fight when you're hardest hit, --
It's when things seem worst that you mustn't quit.

-- Author Unknown --

"Quitting is not an option" is the phrase that stuck with me throughout my college career. I was enrolled in Stonecliff College Online back in 2006. I had been out of high school for about nine years at the time and was really struggling with the thought of failing. Online work was new to me and many of my fellow classmates. We were worried about logging in on time, how to post our assignments in the correct place and most of all balancing work, home, church, and school. We were a mess. We emailed each other and the instructor constantly, reminding him that some of us have been out of school for over ten years and begged him to please be lenient with us when it came to grading our assignments. Finally one of my classmates asked him *"What was your secret to finishing college?"* His answer was simple but very enlightening. If you ask most people what was their secret to success in college they go on to give you this long list of things that will guarantee your success like: study hard, get in a study group, make index cards, and study, study, study, study. But this professor's answer was honest and simple: *"Tenacity."* *"Tenacity?"* we thought. *"What do you mean by tenacity?"* He went on to explain that quitting was not an option for him. No matter how difficult things got for him he was not going to quit. That is what made him successful in his college career. He further stated that many times he had no idea how to do the assignment but he would still just turn something in. When asked by fellow classmates how he knew to do the assignment that way he would say "I didn't I just turned something in. I took his advice and it is what got me through as well. After being out of school for so long you have a tendency to want to be perfect on every assignment and get every answer correct. You even have anxiety about getting one answer wrong. I think subconsciously we don't want to "blow our chances" the second time around. However our instructor told us even if you don't think its right turn something in anyway. Surprisingly when I followed his advice I would get good grades on papers and assignments I thought I did wrong.

We all will have problems that will attempt to side track us from time to time but we mustn't quit. The poem reads "When things go wrong as they sometime will and the road you're trudging seems all uphill....." That indicates that in life we will have problems and things will arise that will be difficult to handle; as another instructor pointed out when I was giving him an excuse as to why I was late turning in one of my assignments. He unsympathetically stated *"unfortunately life happens to us all...."* That's why it is called life. Life is what happens when you have something else planned.

I always wanted to be somebody. From the time I was little I knew I was going to be somebody. I had dreams of being a singer and performer. I would spend hours alone listening to my father's old records. I would write out the words to the songs and then play the record back and sing along with whomever was singing. I imagined I had an audience and I would get up there and sing my heart out. I would even get some of my cousins and friends from the neighborhood and try to start up a singing group. Needless to say it didn't work out the way I planned. But anyhow I was going to be a famous singer, dancer and all around performer. In high school I joined the marching band and participated in talent shows with different dance groups. I got such an adrenaline rush from performing in front of large crowds and to hear them cheer when we were done was the icing on the cake. It was my calling. After high school I had plans to go on the college, then after college I was going to be somebody great. But nobody told me about "LIFE."

My father died when I was about eight years old and I knew absolutely nothing about being a man. My mom did not finish high school or go to college so she honestly couldn't help me with college enrollment. All of a sudden I was out of high school and entering into the real world. All I knew was that the next step was to go to college because that is what you are taught all through school. *"Work hard, get good grades, go on to college, and be successful."* That was the plan to success. But the school system rarely teaches you about "LIFE"; the in between. I remember watching one of Tyler Perry's movies when I heard one of the characters ask "Madea" what happened to this woman who she had grown up with who had so many plans and dreams for her life, but was now strung out on drugs. The character "Madea" replied

"Life honey. Life is what happens when you have something else planned."

After high school I went off to Basic Training with the Army Reserves. This was a great experience for me. I got to get out of Mound Bayou, MS and see another part of the world. I met a lot of different people from different backgrounds and nationalities and I was enjoying every minute of it; except for the whole drill sergeant yelling down your throat part.

After basic and AIT training with the Army Reserves I returned home to Mississippi. It was during the middle of the fall semester of college so I decided to enroll in the spring semester at The Community College in Moorehead, MS. That's when "Life" began to happen. When time came for me to enroll in college I didn't have any transportation and at the time I didn't know anyone who was driving to Moorehead every day. So enrollment came and went the spring semester and still no college. I ended up getting a job at Retail store in Shelby, MS stocking shelves and later at McCarty's Pottery in Merigold, MS. Coming up to the fall semester the following year my brother bought an old beat up Oldsmobile. I talked him into letting me use it to go to school every day. I was finally enrolled in college and driving to Moorehead, MS every day for school. That is until the old car broke down and I had to withdraw from school leaving me with another hurdle to overcome. However I did not quit. I was not taking no for an answer. No matter what life threw at me I was determined to go to college and after nine full years of trying unsuccessfully to enroll, I finally got in; things were finally working in my favor.

Key #3

Walk in Humility

I was in Biology class one evening and it became clear to me that it was possible that my instructor received her degree from a Cracker Jack box. We were in class discussing the process the caterpillar goes through to become a butterfly (metamorphosis). Which I thought was first grade material. The instructor stumbled through the stages clearly not knowing what she was talking about so I proudly broke in and said "first comes the caterpillar, then comes the cocoon, and finally the caterpillar breaks out of the cocoon and becomes a beautiful butterfly." The instructor then looked at me and said "No I don't think that's it." I immediately got a check in my spirit letting me know to agree quickly. I quickly said "you know I think you're right," but unfortunately it was too late. I had tried to correct my instructor in front of the entire class. So at the end of the semester when "A's" were **_"Given"_** out (because we didn't do enough work to earn them), I got a "B." I knew that I had done more work than some of the other students who just showed up occasionally for class, and they all got "A's." Lesson learned.

I had put my foot in my mouth. From that point on I learned to humble myself. I had to understand that while some instructors welcomed correction, or a friendly discussion, others will not tolerate it. Some see it as you trying to undermine them.

The truth is in fact I'm grateful to have received that "B" in biology that semester. I had an overloaded schedule again and if we had received a ton of homework in there I would have been pulling my hair out anyway. I learned very quickly to pay attention and hang onto every word my instructors spoke. I took notes and made my instructors feel like I was really interested in what they were talking about even if they were boring. I learned that saying yes sir and yes Ma'am can turn that D at the end of the semester into a "C" or that "C" into a "B." I realized that my instructors could have really piled on the work if they felt like it and for me to try to show boat and act like a know-it-all was not cool. Apparently she knew something; she had already earned her bachelor's degree while I was still struggling to earn an associate's degree.

The Lord knows I was terrible at math. I took college algebra online and failed miserably. So I decided to take it in the evenings at the high school. I was so lost and for many days I was very frustrated. I hadn't taken algebra since the ninth grade and if it hadn't been for a remedial course which combined the two grades together I would have failed it then too. But I was attentive in class. When the instructor was working the equations out on the board I would ask questions and pretend to be amazed at the answer he gave. When he asked for class participation I would answer the little part I did know like: "a negative times a negative equals a positive." Honestly almost every homework assignment we had I got a

"D" or lower and clearly by the grace of God I got a "C" on the final exam. I was respectful to the instructor and never complained about how fast he worked the problems on the board. I just copied down everything he wrote on the board and stayed out of his way. At the end of the semester when grades were posted I had a "B" in College Algebra. God be praised!

Key #4

Take One Step at a Time

I would advise anyone not be in a rush to get a degree. Enjoy your experience. Even though the ultimate goal is to earn a degree don't let it make you miss out on the college experience itself. College is a time to meet new people, try new things, and most importantly LEARN new lessons. I have known people who, in a quest for a degree, learned absolutely nothing but how to cheat and get other people to do their assignments for them. I have seen some people on one of the famous social networks bragging about their latest achievement of earning a Master's degree. In the same sentence they misspelled words, used words in the wrong context, and broke verbs left to right. My third grade niece spelled better than them. I wondered "how in the world did they earn a Master's Degree in anything." I knew that if they couldn't spell and use words in the right context there is no way they could have read those huge college textbooks or completed their own thesis paper. I was actually upset. Here I was struggling to even get in school and here is this person taking their education for granted by possibly paying someone to do their work for them. Now don't get me wrong. I'm sure we all have used the occasional copy sheet or asked a fellow classmate for an answer during test time. But paying someone to do your work is not going to cut it. Take your time. Do your own work. In the long run it will pay off. If you cheat you are only cheating yourself and your future employer.

Earn your degree. If the Lord blesses you to a point where you don't have to work full time and go to school **Please** take full advantage of the free time you have to study. Nothing bothers me more than seeing someone who does not have to work a full time job sit around, be lazy and fail classes. I worked full time (getting up at 4:30 a.m. to pray and have devotion with God before starting my day), operated a small sandwich business on Wednesdays, remained faithful in church, prepared income taxes, and went to school at night and still got "A's" and "B's." But it was tough. Many days I was so tired I wanted to break down, scream and cry but I was determined to get my education. I had no time for study groups and I rarely had time in between work and school to make it home to do assignments or study before class that evening. I did everything by myself. I earned every grade I got if not by studying hard I earned it by the many sleepless nights I stayed up typing research papers, studying for accounting and pulling my hair out over the dreaded Business Calculus.

I urge all young people, PLEASE take full advantage of your education while you are young. The older you get, the more responsibilities you will have and the more responsibilities you have the more stress you'll have. Many days I went to work dead tired. My coworkers kept saying "*I don't know how you do all you do*" or "*You got too much going on.*" But I was determined to get my education while I still had some youth left. I also had to learn to take my time. A community college is a two year institution and I was determined to graduate on time.

Usually during the first semester advisors recommend that you only take twelve hours so you won't get overwhelmed by all your course work. So the first semester I took twelve hours and got a 3.7 GPA. Next semester I thought I was ready so I signed up for nineteen credit hours which is six classes all mixed in with a full time work schedule, selling sandwiches on Wednesdays, preparing income taxes, and going to church on Wednesday nights. I thought I could handle the load but I ended up failing at least one class every time I signed up for too many. I was trying to hurry up and graduate but was barely learning anything because most days I was too tired to retain the information. My point is "don't rush." The most important thing is that you make it to the end of the journey not how fast you get there. Always remember that whenever you rush you usually end up leaving something valuable behind.

Key #5
Allow angels to work on your behalf

There are angels all around us. These angels are particularly active in the lives of those who are in the perfect will of God. When making decisions in life you want to always know that you are in the perfect will of God. There is a perfect will of God as well as a permissive will of God. The perfect will of God means that you are exactly where God wants you to be whether it seems good or bad to you at the time. In the perfect will of God there may be suffering, you may feel uncomfortable, you may have enemies all around you but you must remain in that position until God releases you or you will have to face that same situation over and over again until you get what God is trying to teach you in that season.

It was hard for me growing up in the Mississippi Delta but I thank God I had angels present all around me. I was smart coming up in elementary school. In the first through the third grade I made the honor roll every nine weeks. My father even went out and bought me a bike. However at the end of my third grade year my father got ill and died. Life had become tough so I began doing just enough to get by. I became an angry kid and somewhat of a bully. I also began talking back to teachers and other adults. Deep down I was hurting and angry. I was angry that my father had died and life had become hard.

I was teased a lot in elementary and Junior High School. I felt I had no one to talk to about what I was going through so I held a lot in. I never learned how to fight and due to my effeminate nature my punches probably wouldn't have done much harm anyway. I often thought "if I could only fight I can keep them from talking about me all the time." I would be walking down the hall or outside playing when someone would start teasing me. I would get so angry but I didn't know what to do about it. So I hung my head and kept walking. I began to avoid crowds of people and eventually became a loner. I no longer fit in.

I often look back on my life and wonder how I made it through all of that. But if I look hard enough I will see that I had angels around me all the time. Even after high school angels were with me. After college didn't work out I got completely off track. I got into the permissive will of God. The permissive will of God is something God allows to happen but He is there looking out for you while you go down this wrong path. I fell into depression and was going to clubs every weekend. I started drinking and smoking marijuana everyday all day. I was hanging out with the wrong crowd and had lost all focus. All I knew was that I wanted to do something with my life but I did not even know where to begin and I didn't want to listen to anyone. I later moved to Memphis, TN after getting a job at one of the casinos that had recently migrated to Robinsonville, MS. I wanted to get out there in the world and make something out of my life. Unfortunately I was carrying some unhealthy baggage. I had a friend who was a "moocher" and was pulling me down. I let this friend talk me into getting an apartment that was too expensive, paying down on a car that I couldn't afford, and going places I had no business going. Many days I went hungry because all of my money went on rent, car note, bills, and gas to get back and forth to work. Some days I had to drive home to Mississippi just to get a meal. But I was determined to be somebody and make something of myself. Things got so bad that I thought I was going to have a nervous breakdown. Then there came an angel. *Psalm 91:11 For He shall give His angels charge over thee to keep thee in all thy ways.*

At the time I was working for the Grand casino as a cage cashier. I became friends with one of the black jack dealers who introduced me to his mother who happened to be a minister. She was a very sweet lady who opened her heart and home to me. She would tell me how special I was to God and how much God loved me and wanted to use me in a mighty way. No one had ever told me anything like that especially about God wanting to use me. She got my attention and I began to visit her home more and more. She also told me that God was going to bring a separation between me and someone in my life that didn't mean me any good. I knew exactly who she was talking about. She would pray with me and I asked would she mind teaching me about God and the bible. She did what she could but she encouraged me to find a church home where I could be taught the ways of God. Well, God did exactly what she said He would. After a huge physical fight between me and my roommate at the apartment complex, I moved out and enrolled at The University of Memphis. I moved into the dormitory the following semester and stayed on campus. I don't quite know why or how but I lost contact with this woman. I slowly began to visit different churches. I was thirsty for something but didn't quite know what it was. While at the University of Memphis I read my bible, went to class, and was enjoying the semester. That is until I lost my job at the casino. My funds had run out on my "tiger card" so I no longer had money for food. I would scrape up the change from between my car seats to buy a bag of twenty-five cent potato chips and a twenty-five cent cake which was my only meal for the day. I would sometime drive home and stock up on ramen noodles and bologna, but because I had no refrigerator I had to eat the bologna before it spoiled. When the semester was over I moved back home to Mississippi. I joined a local church and got re-baptized as an adult who believed in Jesus Christ. I was now back in the perfect will of God and things began to look up from there. I got a part time job working at a thrift store making minimum wages. My car was eventually repossessed so I paid down on a jeep Cherokee which I couldn't afford and had to ask my brother to take over the notes for me. I wanted so badly to quit this lousy thrift store job but I knew I would be outside the perfect will of God again. I experienced a lot of lost before I ever saw any gain. I was stripped down to nothing but the clothes on my back. I had moved back in with my mother and was dependent on her for food and transportation. I rode to church with my boss from the thrift store. I was totally co-dependent and for a time it was very uncomfortable -but necessary. I later came before a prophet who told me that God had allowed it to save me from myself. I was headstrong therefore when I set my mind to do something I was going to do it no matter what.

I was in the perfect will of God at the time. I made just enough money every two weeks to give my mother something on a bill, pay my tithes, give an offering, and buy snacks. Had I earned more I probably would have bought a car and moved away to California or tried to get my own place. But God allowed it and through it He also humbled me and taught me to be content in whatever place or position I found myself. I learned as the song writer penned "the safest place in the whole wide world is in God's will."

Key # 6

Don't worry about things you have no control over

Proverbs 3:5-6 Trust in the Lord with all thine heart and lean not unto thine own understanding. 6. In all thy ways acknowledge Him and He shall direct thy path.

"Lord what do I do now? Lord where do I go from here? Lord, who do I talk to;" are all prayers I have prayed in my quest for an education. Honestly speaking, sometimes it is good not knowing. Not knowing gives you the opportunity to seek God for His plan for your life.

I have known people who have gone to college for four years to become teachers only to discover that they dislike children. I would recommend anyone to go before God and ask *"Lord, what do you think I should major in in college?"* There is absolutely nothing wrong with saying I have no idea what to major in. The only reason I knew what to major in was because I had received so many prophecies about owning my own business. The only major I found in the college catalog dealing with business ownership was Business Administration. I would hate for anyone to waste four, six or eight years of their lives studying for something they may not even like. I would advise anyone to seek God first. I'd suggest going to a pastor, aunt, cousin or someone whom you know can get a prayer through to God. Tell them that you are seeking God's will concerning your education and would like to know His opinion about the situation. Then simply "trust." Don't wait to hear an audible voice from God saying, *"PETER I WANT YOU TO MAJOR IN CRIMINAL JUSTICE!" (However God does speak to some in an audible voice).* Simply trust that just because you acknowledged God (wanted to know his opinion concerning a situation), He is going to direct your path even if it means not this semester or this year. Even if it means not this college but that University and even if it means not that roommate or not that fraternity.

    I was beginning my last semester at community college and only needed one class to graduate. I had taken this class the semester before online and failed it. During the winter break I began seeking God for His plan for the following semester. Graduation was coming up in May of that year and if I passed this class I would be graduating and would have earned an Associates of Arts Degree in Business Administration. My options were to retake the Calculus class online or drive to campus thirty minutes away for class everyday during my lunch break. I chose the second option. Unfortunately it proved to be too stressful. I had to leave work, come home change into decent clothing, drive thirty minutes to an hour long class, then drive thirty minutes back, change back into my work clothes, grab a quick meal, then drive fifteen minutes back to work.

After about the second week the Lord set me down during my time of devotion and said, "Why are you trying so hard to earn that Associate's Degree when the Bachelor's Degree is the one you need?" I then began to weep. I had worked so hard trying to earn that degree and graduating in May would have been the reward for such hard work. I had been at this two-year college now for three and a half years and if I would have retaken the calculus class it would have been four. He then said, "Why not just go on and register with the University that is only ten miles away from your house next semester and begin working towards your bachelor's degree." I was relieved and saddened at the same time; relieved because I could finally rest for a few months and sad because I really wanted to graduate. I didn't realize just how worn out I was. I had lost a lot of sleep and had gained a lot of weight which was having a negative effect on my health. I had gotten so far away from God that I could no longer feel His presence during church services because I had neglected my spiritual responsibilities. I was angry and frustrated with family members and coworkers all of the time. I would cry out to God in frustration saying "Lord I need a break. I need to get away!!!"

Little did I know was that this was exactly what He was doing. I had been in school, working, trying to run a business and maintain spiritual responsibilities for the past three years without any type of vacation whatsoever. I was exhausted and on the verge of a nervous breakdown and didn't even realize it. God had my best interest at heart. Perhaps if I had gone that extra semester I may not be here to tell my story. I realized that God is the creator of the heavens and the earth and sees everything even way up the road.

He sees that the College you are trying to go to this semester is going to lose the accreditation next year and your credits won't be transferable to a University. He sees that the roommate you chose is going to steal all of your clothes while you're away for the weekend or that fraternity you want to pledge is going to lose their charter because of unethical hazing practices. God sees all and He knows all. You can trust that He won't lead you in the wrong direction.

Key #7

Trust in God's Provision

I remember my first semester at community college. As I stated earlier I was totally lost. In the registration process something happened with my financial aid where I could not afford all of my books for class. I also didn't have enough money to pay the two hundred plus dollars for a new book I needed for my Western Civilization course. So I ended up with no textbook for my online class. I borrowed a book from my sister in law but it was a previous edition and needless to say I failed the class that semester; but I didn't give up. I remember a time in my life where something as small as not having a book would have caused me to quit school completely, but this time was different. God was for me this time. He gave me the strength to hang in there and complete the semester. I was secretly hoping that some miracle would happen where I could pass the class without the book. The miracle didn't come that semester. However, I retook the class the following semester, got enough financial aid to buy all my books and had enough left over to get a twelve hundred dollar refund. Oh! By the way, I got an "A" in Western Civilization that semester.

Textbooks can be quite expensive, some costing as much as three to four hundred dollars. However there is a solution to the textbook dilemma. If you don't want to buy high priced textbooks then there are websites out there where you can go to rent your textbooks for a very small amount of money. You just have to remember to mail the book back at the end of the semester so you won't be charged full price. They are also much cheaper on Amazon.com as well. My point in this chapter is this; the Lord will provide us with everything we need for our education. He is our Father and we can always go to Him and say, *"Father I need a book for my "English Composition" course. It costs one hundred fifty dollars and I need it by –* (whatever date class starts.) *Will you provide me with a way to get this book, in Jesus' name?"* The bible states "we have not because we ask not." It also states "ask and you shall receive." And in another place "whatsoever you ask in Jesus name I will do it so that the father may be glorified in the Son." If we don't ask we cannot expect to receive what we need. It's like this, you have a son who needs a poster for school to do a history assignment but he doesn't come to you and ask you to buy the materials needed. The child ends up failing the assignment and when the "F" is brought home you ask *"how did you get an "F"?* The child says *"because I didn't do a history poster board."* Then you say *"What poster board?"* He finally tells you *"I needed one last week but I didn't ask you to buy me one because I didn't want to bother you."* That's how it is with our Heavenly Father. He is concerned with every aspect of our lives; even the smallest details. He longs for us to ask Him for the things we need in life. He also longs to provide those needs for us. It gives Him such joy when His children brag on their Father because He made a way for them to get their supplies for school. When God supplies our needs we are to give Him the Glory (which means tell others of His goodness). You will make Him so proud.

Key #8

Stay in God's Will

As I have mentioned before, the safest place in the whole wide world is in God's will. Always seek to be in the perfect will of God at all times. We are not wise enough to choose our own path. With the way the economy is going you really don't know what jobs will be available in the future. One of the most secure jobs in the world has been threatened with layoffs. That job is the job of a teacher. Almost anyone can become a teacher if he or she can pass the board certifications. Surprisingly many people simply take the easy way out. They major in Education, because the classes are relatively easy. But again, what if you don't like children? You pass all of the necessary courses and get board certified, only to end up realizing you hate your job. Taking the easy way out causes the students you teach to be neglected because you don't have a passion for what you do. You simply do enough to maintain a steady paycheck. You yell all of the time, speak curses over the children, and complain about everything. Not because you are a bad person but because you are not anointed to be a teacher. You are out of position. Your destiny may have been to become a lawyer or a physical therapist but because the curriculum was relatively easy and you could be finished in as little as four years you coped out. Now you are miserable. If you are destined to be a doctor or a physical therapist go back to school and *Take Your Time*. Even if it takes you six more years to complete your degree **Go For It**. You will be much happier.

When I first graduated from high school I enrolled at a community college in Moorehead, MS and was majoring in Electronics Technology. I didn't even know what that was, but because it looked easy and I could be finished in two years I selected this as my major. I had the idea that the sooner you get a degree the sooner you could get a good job making good money and then live happily ever after. After all that's what happens in the movies right?

I knew a guy who did the exact same thing. He went to this community college and majored in welding. If you knew him you knew that he was not cut out for any type of dirty work. Yet because it was easy and could be completed in as little as two years he went for it. He graduated and got a job welding. Although he made good money he only lasted about six months. He was clearly not cut out for this type of work. The moral is you want to seek God for His purpose for your life. You have a destiny and it can only be unlocked or discovered by a true and living God. You have a purpose and a destiny. We all are destined to be SOMEBODY. We all have a purpose in this life. Everybody is not destined to be the next Jennifer Hudson. Some of us are destined to be her assistant. Some of us are destined to be her house keeper; to keep the limo clean; to keep the garden fresh; to operate the restaurant where she goes to eat with family and friends. We are not all meant to be in the spotlight. Some of the greatest work happens behind the scenes. Take Whitney Houston for example. When she steps out on the stage to sing or speak she looks flawless. Guess what? Someone has to do her hair, make-up and wardrobe. Your sole purpose in life may be to make someone else look good. Please don't get into jealousy. **You** be the best hairdresser, make-up artist or designer you can be.

The reason we are sometime so unhappy is because we are doing something we were never supposed be doing in the first place. If I would have majored in electronics technology there is no telling where I would be today. Sometime God causes us to wait a few years before going to college but no matter how long it takes seek to remain in God's perfect will because timing is everything. Go before God and say *"Lord who am I destined to be?" I want to be a _____ but it is hard and takes too long. I want to take the easy way out. Please help me to discover my destiny Lord. They tell me my destiny is found in you. Please lead me in the right path even if it means waiting a few years until it is my season to do what you have called me to do, in Jesus Name."*

Key #9

Get out of God's Way

God knows us all pretty well. He knows what it will take to get us from point "A" to point "B." Our trials and tribulations are the tools God often uses to make us. If I would have gone on to college immediately after high school with the same attitude I had my life would have ended up a lot worse than it was. I had absolutely no respect for authority. I was a spoiled brat. I usually got my way. I did almost whatever I wanted when I wanted to do it. I was also stubborn and rebellious. I didn't want to listen to anything anybody had to say. I knew it all and you were stupid to try to tell me anything different.

I felt like such a failure all those years I tried unsuccessfully to get into college. I thought there was something wrong with me and of course I beat up on myself every minute for it. I also blamed everyone else for not doing some part that I thought they were supposed to have done to support me. I had to learn humility fast; and what better place to learn humility than in the real world. As I stated earlier I was very proud. I had an opinion of myself that was too high. I thought I was someone I was not. I was living a fairytale life. I had watched a little too much T.V. and had become a DIVO (a male version of a DIVA). I looked down on others and found fault in everyone else when all along I was the one with the problem. I said things without regard to the feelings of others and I always wanted the top position no matter who I hurt to get it. I once stole a job from one of my former classmates.

My cousin picked me up while I was walking one day and in the car with him was one of our classmates. They were on their way to a job interview and this other person in the car was promised the position. We all went in the store but he was a little shy about asking for the manager, so being the bold person that I was I went and asked about the position and needless to say I ended up getting the job. I had stolen a job from this guy who really needed it because he was scheduled to go to college in the fall and needed the extra money for clothing and supplies. The woman asked "did so-and-so send you?" I said no. Then she asked "how did you hear about the position?" I told her I overheard someone talking about it and I ended up with the position. That was so ugly of me. Years later I called this classmate who is now the principal of a school here in Mississippi and apologized for the wrong I had done toward him. He said *"you know what Cedric I had forgotten all about that, and who knows where I would be if I would have taken that job. I may not be where I am today."* I felt a sense of peace after I had made amends for my wrong and I slowly began to realize that I had issues. I began to take notice of how I treated people and it was not a pretty sight. God had to humble me. I was too proud (the wrong kind of proud). The danger in it all was that I couldn't see it. I now realize that I was not a failure because I was unable to successfully get into college, *I was simply not ready. I had to be broken, remade and put back in the furnace of life until I became a new person.*

Imagine the tyrant I would have been if I were put over a school system with the attitude I had. Imagine how many failed business ventures I would have because I didn't want to take advice from anyone; the last thing anyone wants or needs is a know-it-all boss. Imagine how many jobs I would have been fired from for trying to take the boss' position. God knew exactly what He was doing. I now see why it took so long. *I was not ready.*

I would advise anyone to get out of God's way. He knows exactly what He is doing with our lives. Don't get off track like I did. I saw a lot of my classmates graduating from college and I became anxious. I have student loans to pay off now because I got in God's way. I have had to retake classes that I passed at one college because I could not get a copy of my transcripts due to the fact that I owed them money. The root cause of it all was I got in God's way and out of His timing.

Key #10

Know that you can do it

"I can do all things through Christ which strengtheneth me."Philippians 4:13

"Our deepest fear is not that we are inadequate. Our deepest fear is that we are powerful beyond measure. It is our light, not our darkness that most frightens us. We ask ourselves, Who am I to be brilliant, gorgeous, talented, fabulous? Actually, who are you not to be? You are a child of God. Your playing small does not serve the world. There is nothing enlightened about shrinking so that other people won't feel insecure around you. We are all meant to shine, as children do. We were born to make manifest the glory of God that is within us. It's not just in some of us; it's in everyone. And as we let our own light shine, we unconsciously give other people permission to do the same. As we are liberated from our own fear, our presence automatically liberates others."

—*a poem by Marrianne Williamson*

Is there anything too hard for God? No matter how bad one's life may have been or how low one may think he is on the totem pole, God can make something beautiful out that life. He specializes in extremely difficult cases. God enjoys taking people who others toss aside as useless and cleaning them up. Then he takes these same people and put them on display so the whole world can see his marvelous work. The reason He does this is so that we *"the nobody's"* (according to the world's standards) can have someone to relate to and that He may receive all the glory (credit) for their success.

It blesses me to hear the testimonies of some of our greatest evangelists of today tell how they never went to college yet they are authors, business owners, millionaires, and billionaires. One televangelist who has written countless books went on to tell that she failed English in high school. Then she goes on to say *"look at me now." "Look at what the **Lord** has done."* (It is my belief that knowledge is power and that a good education opens up many doors that otherwise would remain closed.) Yet, many of us have never gone to seminary or even college for that matter. It is sometimes difficult to relate to some of the testimonies given in the big churches of today. (Not to take anything away from those who have studied hard and earned their college degrees.) On top of that, many of us are far from normal. Many of us didn't come from a privileged background. Some of us came up stricken with poverty, learning disabilities, were raped, beaten, and molested. Some, not all, were placed in the special education program undeservingly. But I am so thankful that God has chosen the foolish things of this world to confound the wise;

and God hath chosen the weak things of the world to confound the things which are mighty; *1 Corinthians 1:27*

"Life for me ain't been no crystal stair." I grew up in the country in a family that didn't have a lot of money. I wore my brother's hand me down clothes; we lived in a house where the roof leaked when it rained and another house where if you made a wrong step you could fall through the floor. My father and grandfather raised hogs and if you hung laundry out on a windy day they would reek of hog slop and manure. I didn't really fit in while in school so I got teased constantly. So to keep from being an outsider I began doing whatever I could to fit in. I started drinking, smoking, and even talking back to teachers. I got hooked up with a crowd who were doing the same things and eventually we started skipping school. Needless to say they all dropped out but by the grace of God I graduated in 1997 on time. Sadly, like many teenagers I did almost anything to try to fit in because I hated being teased. However, I was actually smart. I also had a lot of talent but listening to what others said about me caused me to walk in constant fear and inferiority.

During my first semester at the community college in Clarksdale, MS some people could see that I was different. They could see the anointing on my life and would call me out; not in a bad way but they would tell others that I was a preacher. I however did not want anyone knowing that I was called to be a minister; partly because I wasn't licensed or ordained as a minister and the other reason was I didn't want to stand out. I wanted to fit in with everyone else because I knew from experience and from reading the bible that being different brings persecution. I was comfortable sitting quietly at my desk like everyone else. I managed to get by at the community college without persecution because I did a real good job at fitting in. After a while I began to dress like everyone else and was very careful not to do anything to reveal my true identity.

Sadly on my job it was a totally different story. I could not hide or fit in because my boss knew that I was a minister. She then told her boss and all the workers I was a minister. I learned that when one is truly anointed he cannot hide it. The anointing is sweet and it draws people. Unfortunately it also draws attacks from the enemy. However I had to be taught that the attacks are never about me but about the anointing of God that rests upon my life. The anointing destroys yokes and removes burdens. And because the anointing is the presence of God resting upon one's life demons get nervous when you enter a room. When the anointing of God rests upon a person's life it is virtually impossible to hide out or fit in. Someone will always notice that there is something different about you.

God gave me favor on my job. Psalm 5:12. Most days I was simply being myself. I didn't bother anyone, I just showed up and laughed and made others laugh and unknowingly became the center of attention. I was "different" and because I was "different" I was not liked very well by a few of my coworkers. I had not given them a reason not to like me. They simply didn't like me. One lady would go home and tell her family about me and they would get upset because she was always talking about "Cedric said this and Cedric said that." She said one of her family members said about me that "nobody can be that happy all of the time." We had a big laugh and I told her she'd better stop talking about me to her folks before we both get jumped on. I also had known my boss for a number of years and she was the one who informed me about the job opening both times I was hired there. She also helped me out a lot when I was going to school. She was generous enough to let us use her truck when we moved and on several occasions she gave me money for gas and on top of that she always got me and my mother birthday presents. To show our gratitude I would bring her home cooked lunches that my mother cooked daily. Some of the coworkers saw this as me trying to kiss up to the boss. What they didn't realize is that God favored me. If one looks with the natural eye it may very well look like the boss is showing favoritism. However what my coworkers did not understand is that when God favors a person, things will never seem fair; because favor isn't fair. Whether I ever brought her anything or not I would still have favor because favor does not come from man. It comes from God.

Whenever a new person was hired someone would grab hold to them and proceed to tell them about "Cedric" and how

"Cedric" doesn't do this and how "Cedric" doesn't do that. I had an idea to start a sandwich shop about a year after I began working at this job. My pastor asked me to see if I could get Wednesday's off to run the business. I went to the owner and asked to be off on Wednesday's and he gave me the ok. That was God's favor at work once again. Some of my coworkers began to despise me even more. I could even see one of my coworkers snarling at me out of the corner of my eye when I would be working. (He still does it to this day). I laugh and just thank God.

God had really blessed me. I was in college, I wore nice clothes, I sold sandwiches on Wednesdays and during the winter months I prepared income taxes. When one car would break down on me God would bless me with another one. For the past few years God has blessed me to have two cars in the driveway paid for in full. However my biggest downfall was that I gave my testimony to the wrong people. I even became a little braggadocio. I learned the hard way that I shouldn't have shared how God had blessed me with everyone because not everyone was excited to see me prosper. I had been told this before but for some reason I was still naïve enough to think that everyone was going to be just as excited as I was about the blessings of God. I learned that often times if one person is prospering more than another, the Spirit of Jealousy may rise up and cause the one to hate or even attempt to do bodily harm to the other. Jealousy had become hatred and I became despised in the eyes of some of my coworkers. At first I was able to deal with it because I had dealt with this spirit before. Every time my enemies came against me I would bless them. I would also pray for them. There were times when things got better but it didn't last very long. In fact things got so bad that one of my coworkers wanted to physically attack me. He would get everyone together in the back corner of the building and plant seeds of discord against me. It all came to a boil right after my older brother died in a car accident. I was going through the stages grief and at that point I was stuck in the anger stage. This particular enemy picked the wrong time to mess with me. This one guy in particular just kept picking day after day after day and I had taken all I could take. I was about to explode. This particular day, as cowards do, he once again rallied the coworkers in the corner and had a discussion about how much Cedric gets away with and how Cedric doesn't have to do this, and how Cedric doesn't do that. He even got one guy so stirred up that he actually said something to me. We exchanged words and it got to the point where I was about to strike him. Take note that all of this happened while the boss was out of the building. To keep from striking this man I went in the restroom and prayed a "for real" prayer to God. I said *"Lord I'm tired of this man picking at me and if you don't do something I'm going to "bust his head!!!. "Lord I surrender. Please do something. I'm not strong enough right now handle this situation on my own. I give it over to you."*

The Holy Spirit then impressed upon me to tell my boss about the incident as soon as she came back in the building. We were cleaning up for the day and getting ready to begin our weekend. As we were clocking out for the day my boss was returning. I was still boiling with rage when I decided to tell her about what was going on. She said she would talk it over with her boss and they would deal with the situation. Monday morning came and the situation was dealt with. Everyone was called near the time clock and was told in so many words not to worry about what other people were doing and to focus on one's own responsibilities. Then she said to me, *"if they give you any more trouble you let me know and I'm going to send them home for three days."* After she asked did I have anything to say she asked me to lead the group in prayer. PRAISE The Lord!!! God stepped in and resolved the situation. Not long after that the guy was transferred to another department.

I wanted to include this chapter because I want my readers to be comfortable with being themselves. I had to learn that everyone has haters and not everyone is going to like me no matter how much I kiss up and try to fit in. I used to be such a compromiser even after I got saved. My pastor once told me *"don't expect everybody to like you. Some people will never like you no matter what you do."* And after spending many days and nights crying to God about it He finally gave me the boldness to get over it. I had to get over trying to fit in. I had to learn that I will be hated by some and loved by others.

The bible tells us that we are blessed when men revile us and persecute us and say all manner of evil against us because of the name of Christ. Matthew 5:11. The question for me was "Can you stand to be blessed?!!!"

One can be and do whatever God has called him to do. However one is deceived if he thinks everyone will leap for joy because he decides to walk in his destiny. Remember 1John 4:4 *"Ye are of God, little children, and have overcome them: because greater is he that is in you, than he that is in the world."*

Key #11

Have the proper mindset

Depending on the mindset, what is easy to one person can be truly challenging to another. However I didn't realize this until recently. I thought everybody learned at the same pace and that if someone didn't know what I knew then something was wrong with them. It actually aggravated me to be asked a question that I thought was so simple. I would frown and think "are you serious, you don't know that simple answer?" I was unknowingly a snob. I wanted to be somebody so badly that I often looked down on people I thought were nobodies. I was what one calls an arrogant fault finder. I examined people, located their flaws, and judged them accordingly. Sadly I've missed out on many great relationships because of this evil spirit called pride (an opinion of oneself that is too high).

I erroneously thought I was better than everyone else. Yet I was toughest on myself. I have called myself weak, stupid, lazy, and a failure. I didn't realize I wasn't perfect nor was I expected to be perfect. There is so much that I don't know yet often I am too proud to ask for help because I have erroneously thought that I had to have all the answers and if I didn't know everything then something was wrong with me. I have heard people say of me 'he think he knows everything" or "you can't tell him nothing." I did not realize that all of this time I had a serious pride problem. I thank God for brokenness. I could not be the man I am today without my seasons of brokenness.

Some would have us believe that college is "so" difficult. That one must be a literal genius to excel in college. The truth that I have experienced is college is not hard at all. The key is learning how to and making time to study. Though we all learn at a different pace, we all are capable of learning. Chances are if one can read he can study also. Depending on the major, college is no harder than high school. It may take learning better study skills or even a tutor, yet college is for you if you really want to go. The same thing one does to pass high school is the same thing he is going to need to do to pass in college. Except college requires a lot more discipline. More than likely mom and dad won't be around to force us to study and there will be many distractions. Some type of study schedule has to be made where you will be free from distraction for a certain length of time. During this time it is very important that the cell phone is turned off because those social networks and text messages from friends will be huge distractions.

Most Orientation courses teach study skills and the different learning styles so it is very important to pay attention in this class. It is almost impossible to learn something if you do not go over the material. With many college courses people confuse difficult with poor time management. What happens in some cases is a student doesn't take the time to study the material then if they fail they begin complaining to others about how difficult the class was. The truth is not enough time was set aside to go over the material. I used pray and ask God for a miracle when I didn't study for tests and was often disappointed when I failed. I had to learn that "if I didn't put anything in I couldn't get anything out." I simply needed to study.

If the class is offered as a part of the curriculum then it can be passed. Again that is why I strongly recommend a student take Orientation their first semester and really pay attention. Discovering, learning, and developing a good study habit will make all the difference in succeeding in college.

I also like to advise students that are fresh out of high school to go on and get their education before they have too many responsibilities. Chances are the longer one waits the more responsibilities he may take on and the harder it may be to make time to study.

I cannot begin to tell about the many nights I had to stay up all night studying and doing assignments. I wouldn't go to bed most nights until three o'clock in the morning and then had to get back up at four thirty to prepare for work. I worked all day while periodically falling asleep standing up at my work station, then had to rush home at three or four o'clock to prepare last minute homework for my next class at five and six o'clock that evening. Most days I only got about four hours of sleep. I would have learned so much more if I only had the time. I completed my assignments and turned them in but I could have done much better and have gotten so much more out of the lessons if I only had more time and less responsibility.

Key #12

Learn to ask for help

Asking for help was one area in my life that I struggled with. It was probably one of the hardest lessons I had learn. I was a mama's boy growing up and I was used to my mama doing everything for me. My mother defended me from bullies and family members who teased me and called me out of my name. She really spoiled me. However there was an area that she couldn't help me with and that was how to be a man. After high school I needed guidance. There are some things that a mother can't teach a man. I was lost and since most of my family hadn't gone to college or finished high school for that matter I felt that they couldn't help me. I needed help and as a man I needed a role model to pattern my life after but I found none. Most of the men I knew were either dead, alcoholics, or hadn't achieved any type of success in their lives.

As I stated earlier I always wanted to be somebody. I desperately wanted to get out of Mississippi and into the world and make something out of myself. However I was missing the basics like: (1) after high school there were no free lunches or free bus rides to school; (2) mama was no longer obligated to buy me clothes, (3) when I finished high school I was now on my own, and I needed a job to support myself, (4) I needed a car to get back and forward to work and/or school and (5) and that the ultimate purpose of getting an education was so that I could get a better job to support myself. I did not know the importance of a job so I had no problem quitting one job to go get another.

I had to learn early that no one owed me anything. My parents were only obligated to take care of me until I graduated from high school. If for any reason I decided not to finish school the contract became void. If I dropped out in the ninth grade I would be telling my parents that I obligated myself to get a job to take care of my responsibilities; to buy my own clothes, help out on the bills, and pay rent if I had to.

For a while I blamed others as the reason I was not doing anything with my life. I used the excuse *"If my mother would have been harder on me I would be a lot further in life."* For a while I failed to take responsibility for my own bad choices. For years I played the blame game, but I had to realize that it was not my mother's fault that I was not where I felt I should've been in life. I was ultimately responsible for fulfilling my own destiny.

I used to always have to have someone to go places with me and ask the questions I was afraid to ask, but God gave me the boldness to begin to ask for myself. I had to stop depending on others to do everything for me and take responsibility for my own life. In time things began to work out in your favor. So I learned the big lesson "nobody owes me anything." It was time for me to man up; lace up my boot straps, gird up my loins, and face life head on. I had to forgive the people who hurt and disappointed me. I had to grow up and stop being mad at people for something they did or didn't do when I was twelve years old. I had to get over it, move on, and step up and be the man that I was destined to be. To do this I would have to learn to ask for help on my own. I had to learn that I was not dumb, stupid, or lazy because I needed help. I had been out of high school for a long time and I needed help. So I started asking a lot of questions. I wanted to go back to college so I contacted the school and just started asking questions. Sometimes I wouldn't ask the right question or my question would be misunderstood so I began writing my questions down before calling. Gradually I began getting the right answers to my questions and I learned that it gets easier each time you do it.

Would you like to see your manuscript become a book?

If you are interested in becoming a PublishAmerica author, please submit your manuscript for possible publication to us at:

acquisitions@publishamerica.com

You may also mail in your manuscript to:

**PublishAmerica
PO Box 151
Frederick, MD 21705**

We also offer free graphics for Children's Picture Books!

www.publishamerica.com